AN AVALANCHE OF MURDER

A full-length comic mystery by
Matt Buchanan

www.youthplays.com
info@youthplays.com
424-703-3515

CAST OF CHARACTERS

ARTIE (Arthur Hopkins, Jr.), 38. Investment banker. Husband of Virginia, son of Arthur and Muriel, nephew of Gloria, father of Mary and Anthony, ex-husband of Sharon.

VIRGINIA, 32. Socialite (don't call her Ginny). Third wife of Artie.

ANTHONY, 11. Son of Artie and Sharon, grandson of Arthur and Muriel, great-nephew of Gloria, nephew of Nancy, Mark and Amy, brother of Mary.

MARY, 13. Daughter of Artie and Sharon, granddaughter of Arthur and Muriel, great-niece of Gloria, niece of Nancy, Mark and Amy, sister of Anthony.

ARTHUR (Arthur Hopkins, Sr.), 68. Greeting card writer. Husband of Muriel, father of Artie, Nancy, Mark and Amy, grandfather of Mary and Anthony.

GLORIA, 72. Spinster. Sister of Muriel, aunt of Artie, Nancy, Mark and Amy, great-aunt of Mary and Anthony.

MURIEL, 67. Wife of Arthur, sister of Gloria, mother of Artie, Nancy, Mark and Amy, grandmother of Mary and Anthony.

COLLETTE, 23. Maid to the Hopkins family.

AMY, 24. Fashion model. Daughter of Arthur and Muriel, niece of Gloria, sister of Artie, Nancy and Mark, aunt of Mary and Anthony.

NANCY, 30. English professor. Wife of Harry, daughter of Arthur and Muriel, niece of Gloria, sister of Artie, Mark and Amy, aunt of Mary and Anthony.

HARRY, 49. Bank manager. Husband of Nancy.

MARK, 26. Graduate student. Friend of Betsy, son of Arthur and Muriel, nephew of Gloria, brother of Artie, Nancy and Amy, uncle of Mary and Anthony.

BETSY, 21. College student. Friend of Mark.

*OFFICER ONE, a police officer.

*OFFICER TWO, a police officer.

*SHARON, 35, mother of Mary and Anthony, first (now ex-) wife of Artie.

> (*NOTE: The last three characters make only very brief appearances at the end. They can easily be doubled by the actors playing characters who are dead by then — or they can be played by members of the stage crew.)

SETTING

The entire play takes place in the central living room space of a very, very large, artificially rustic mountain cabin. Exits lead to the kitchen (and back exit beyond), to the front hallway (and front exit beyond), and to the bedrooms, etc. The bedrooms might be upstairs—ideally, there might even be a balcony overlooking the living room, as in a traditional ski lodge. Depends on your budget and your taste. What's important is that folks can disappear in the direction of the bedrooms, in the direction of the kitchen, or in the direction of the front door, and that it be clear in which direction they're heading. If you can afford them, the living room could have windows and a fireplace, and if you really want to pull out all the stops, the windows could be lighted or not to indicate time of day. There should be various forms of seating—couches, easy chairs, a rocker, etc.—scattered about the room in locations that make for strong composition when a large group occupies the space.

ACTING NOTE

Though set in America and in the present day, this play is

intended both as an example of and as an affectionate spoof of the old-fashioned English drawing-room mystery, in which the characters maintain their aplomb, for the most part, even as the body count rises. It will work better if the characters are unaware of the ridiculousness of their reactions. While it is perfectly fine for the characters to display sadness over the loss of loved ones and fear for their own safety, they must go on doggedly trying to solve the mystery even if the actors believe that they themselves would be prostrate with grief or fear in similar circumstances. This is especially true of the actors playing Mary and Anthony.

STYLE NOTE

Again, because this play is meant to be both an example of and a spoof of old-time murder mysteries, the director has wide latitude in style. It will work played perfectly straight, but if you want to add melodramatic touches like musical stingers after "significant" lines, etc., that will work too.

CASTING NOTE

While written as a boy, the role of Anthony may be played instead as a girl named Annie if desired. Simply change the name and any relevant pronouns. Similarly, the small roles of Officer One and Officer Two may be male or female.

ACKNOWLEDGMENT

An Avalanche of Murder was read before an audience in June 2016, by students from Ayer/Shirley High School (Ayer, MA), under the direction of drama teacher JulieAnn Govang. The cast was as follows:

STAGE DIRECTIONS	Jared Magno
ARTIE	Liam Gleason
VIRGINIA	Brooke Martinez
ANTHONY	Deran Quinty
MARY	Julia Alo
ARTHUR	Ryan Messcher
GLORIA	Nadia Nalesnik
MURIEL	Katherine Krieger
COLLETTE	Catherine Quinty
AMY	Vannah Pyatt
NANCY	Leah Robinson
HARRY	Sarah Parrish
MARK	Jared Magno
BETSY	Michelle Woodland
OFFICERS	Nadia Nalesnik
SHARON	Sarah Parrish

(Late afternoon. Lights up on the empty living room. Enter ARTIE, 38, a stuffy investment banker; VIRGINIA, 32, his socialite wife; and their two children, ANTHONY, 11 and MARY, 13; from the front hallway, in their winter outdoor things. They drag suitcases and skis.)

ARTIE: Well, we made it.

VIRGINIA: Finally. Honestly, I don't understand why we have to come on these family outings anyway. Your family is impossible.

ARTIE: Now, dear. We've been over this.

ANTHONY: Dibs on the top bedroom!

(Anthony races through and out of the room [or up the stairs if there are any] towards the bedrooms, pursued by Mary.)

MARY: No way! It's mine!

VIRGINIA: Well, they are! Especially that crazy old man.

ARTIE: That crazy old man is my father, Virginia. He also happens to be the source of the money that buys your designer snowsuits, my dear.

VIRGINIA: Well, but does he have to dress that way? And act that way? I don't know when I was more embarrassed than at that restaurant today. Talking poetry to that waitress!

ARTIE: Well, that's the way he always talks. Comes from making his fortune writing greeting cards, I guess. Eccentric geniuses are like that, dear. But if you want to inherit any of that lovely money of his, you'd better get used to being nice to him anyway.

VIRGINIA: Yes, I know, so you're always saying. It's bad enough I have to put up with those two delinquent kids of yours.

ARTIE: Mary and Anthony are far from delinquent and you

know it. You might at least try to be a mother to them.

VIRGINIA: But I'm <u>not</u> their mother, as Mary is constantly reminding me.

ARTIE: Never mind. She'll come around. Thirteen is a difficult age under any circumstances.

VIRGINIA: Thank goodness they live with their mother most of the time!

ARTIE: Let's get our bags upstairs and start unpacking.

(They exit to the bedrooms. After a moment, enter ARTHUR, 68, the patriarch, who speaks in verse; his wife MURIEL, 67; her crabby unmarried sister GLORIA, 72 and COLLETTE, 23, their French maid; from the front hallway, in their winter outdoor things and carrying luggage. Collette is struggling with the biggest load.)

ARTHUR: *(Rubbing his hands together in the cold:)* So cold outside. But now I feel revived.
I wonder if our children have arrived.

GLORIA: *(Sniffing:)* Judging from the snowy footprints, I'd say they have. And judging from the number and size of the footprints, and the fact that very little attempt seems to have been made to leave the snow on the mat, I'd guess it's my nephew Arthur, Jr. and his two hellions.

MURIEL: Now, dear, do be nice. Anthony and Mary are lovely children.

GLORIA: There's no such thing as lovely children. I'll be in my room, lying down. Collette, you French baggage, bring my bags.

(She stalks off toward the bedrooms, followed by Collette, heavily laden with bags. Arthur watches them go.)

ARTHUR: That lovely speech inspires me to say:

Your sister Gloria's in fine form today.

MURIEL: Oh, be nice.

ARTHUR: The love I bear for you, my dearest wife,
Constrains me to allow her in my life.
But no two sisters are more different.
You know I mean that as a compliment.

MURIEL: *(Giggling:)* I know you do. You know, sometimes I think it's a mistake inviting her to our family get-togethers.

ARTHUR: It's no good not inviting that one, love.
She'd come along despite us, push or shove.

MURIEL: I suppose so. Arthur, do you think she'd be any different if she'd married?

ARTHUR: Perhaps if she'd known love like you and me,
She'd be as nice as anyone could be.
But then, it might be just because she's not
That Gloria has never tied the knot.
And marriage doesn't work for everyone.
It hasn't done much for our eldest son.

MURIEL: Oh, I don't know. Sharon gave Artie two wonderful kids — whatever my sister thinks of them.

ARTHUR: Oh, Sharon is just lovely, true enough.
Too bad she wouldn't stand for all the stuff
That our son Arthur Jr. put her through.
She left him standing, as they mostly do.
This new one, though, Virginia: She's a pill.
I hope she dumps him soon — she probably will.
An awful thing to say. I know, I know.
Pretend I didn't. Now, come on, let's go.

MURIEL: I can't wait to see the grandchildren.

(Arthur kisses Muriel and they exit towards the bedrooms. After

a moment, enter AMY, 24, an up-and-coming fashion model; NANCY, 30, an English professor; and HARRY, 49, her banker husband; from outside as the others.)

AMY: Thanks again for waiting for me at the airport, dear bro-in-law. These photographers can never stay within their time budget. I don't know how I'd have gotten up here if you hadn't waited.

NANCY: And here I thought all you supermodels traveled by chauffeured limo.

AMY: Sorry to disillusion you, sis. And I'm hardly a supermodel. Not yet, anyway. Seriously, though, thanks, you guys. No cab would ever have agreed to come way up here this late in the year.

HARRY: You know, I've been thinking about that. I'm not sure Arthur is right to have this gathering up here this late. Remember five years ago?

AMY: Five years ago I was in Europe, remember? That's when I found Collette working in that dingy carnival and brought her home.

HARRY: Well, there was an avalanche up here. The snow completely blocked the pass. No one could get in or out for weeks. And that was even earlier than it is now.

NANCY: Oh, don't talk about avalanches. The very idea gives me the heebie-jeebies. Come on, let's find our rooms and see who else has arrived.

(They exit towards the bedrooms. After a moment, MARK, 26, a graduate student, and his girlfriend BETSY, 21, enter; like the others in outdoor gear [though Betsy's is a little inadequate for the weather] and lugging suitcases.)

MARK: *(Bowing elaborately:)* Welcome to Hopkins Manor!

BETSY: *(Giggling:)* Oh, wow — is it really called that?

MARK: No — I don't think it's really called anything in particular. Mostly we just say "the lodge."

BETSY: Pretty snazzy. Looks like a chalet out of a James Bond movie.

MARK: SHHH! Don't tell! I'm really Hans Blofeld, supervillain.

BETSY: Meathead! Remind me again why I'm here?

MARK: I want you to meet the family.

BETSY: Will they like me? Or will they think I'm just after the Hopkins fortune?

MARK: Please — they'll love you. It's you I'm worried about. If you're going to marry me, you have a right to know what a family of nuts you'll be getting involved with.

BETSY: Well, I already met your niece and nephew, remember, when we took them to the zoo, and they couldn't be sweeter.

MARK: Yeah, Mary and Anthony are all right, despite my stick-in-the-mud brother. Actually, their mother is great too — she just got tired of Artie and his "secretaries." The present Mrs. Artie is a piece of work.

BETSY: What about the rest of the family? I can't believe I'm so nervous.

MARK: Well, I think you'll like my father. He's got that whole eccentric genius thing going, but he's fun.

BETSY: He's the King of the Greeting Card, right?

MARK: Actually, he's the queen, really, since he writes all his greeting cards under the name "Veronica Hopkins." Apparently bad poetry sells better if it's by a woman.

BETSY: Is he bad?

MARK: Oh, he's terrible, but it seems like he's terrible in just the right way for sappy greeting cards. He's made a small fortune. And, like I say, he's fun. So is Mom, really. My brother Artie—the firstborn—is some kind of banker. Investments or something. He's a real bore, but he's basically harmless. Virginia's his third wife. Whatever you do, don't call her "Ginny." That should tell you a lot. You've met the kids. My sister Nancy is an English professor. She's pretty cool. Her husband Harry's a lot older than she is, but I don't know anything else against him. He's some kind of banker like Artie, but he doesn't let it go to his head. Then there's Amy. You know who she is.

BETSY: I've seen her picture, anyway. In magazines.

MARK: Yeah, she's starting to do all right for herself. She's the baby—basically.

BETSY: What does <u>that</u> mean?

MARK: Well, we don't talk about it much, but I had another sister—Tessie. A year younger than Amy. She disappeared in Paris when she was four. I was seven.

BETSY: Disappeared? You mean you never found her?

MARK: Never.

BETSY: But that's terrible.

MARK: *(Shrugging:)* It was a long time ago. We tried to find her, of course—Mom and Dad hounded the French authorities for at least five years—but eventually you have to move on.

BETSY: It's tragic.

MARK: And that's not the only tragedy. I had another older brother, too. Phillip. At least we know what happened to him.

BETSY: What happened?

MARK: I was nine. Phillie was fifteen. We were at the beach in Australia, on vacation.

BETSY: Oh, my goodness — did a shark eat him?

MARK: No, he got caught in an undertow. The thing was, he knew better, but I didn't. He'd swum out to make _me_ come in. I always felt like it was my fault.

BETSY: You poor thing! You were nine! It wasn't your fault.

MARK: He washed ashore about 75 miles away, so at least we got to bury him. Not like Tessie. It's okay. It was a long time ago.

BETSY: And that's the whole family.

MARK: Yep. Except — dang — Freudian slip! I forgot Aunt Gloria. Aunt Godzilla, we kids used to call her.

BETSY: Why? Does she lay waste to cities?

MARK: If they get in her way, she does. Except lately she's getting so absent-minded she can't really breathe fire anymore. You'll see. I wonder where everybody is. _(Calling out:)_ Hey, anybody home?

> _(With a significant amount of noise [especially if there are stairs], Mary and Anthony come charging on from the bedrooms.)_

MARY: Uncle Mark!

ANTHONY: Hey, Uncle Mark! Hey, Betsy!

> _(Mutual hugs and/or backslapping, etc.)_

MARK: Hey, munchkins. Where is everybody?

> _(Arthur enters from the bedrooms.)_

ARTHUR: We're here, and wondering what could be your

fate.

We might have known you'd be arriving late.

MARK: *(Shaking hands:)* Hey, hey — not late. Just last.

(Muriel enters from the bedrooms.)

MURIEL: Your sister's session ran long and she had to change her flight, and she still beat you here. *(She kisses Mark, then notices Betsy.)* Hello.

MARK: Oh! Sorry! Betsy Macy, this is my mother, Muriel Hopkins and my father, Arthur Hopkins. Mom, Dad — this is Betsy.

BETSY: I'm very pleased to meet you both.

ARTHUR: No more than we. We're glad to have you here. Our son has told us all about you, dear.

MARK: *(Hurriedly:)* All of it good!

ARTHUR: Of course, of course, I hasten now to say. *(Shaking hands:)* So welcome, Betsy. Please enjoy your stay.

MURIEL: Yes, welcome, my dear. I hope you'll enjoy our little family gathering. Let me show you to your rooms. *(Looking at Mark.)* That's rooms, plural.

MARK: Of course! Wouldn't have it any other way!

MURIEL: Right answer, son. *(Giving Besty a wink as she takes the smallest suitcase:)* Children, help your uncle and your future aunt with their bags.

(Anthony and Mary each grab two suitcases and energetically drag them after Muriel toward the bedrooms. Mark and Betsy follow them off, Mark silently mouthing "I'm sorry!" as Betsy giggles. Almost as soon as they're gone, Amy sweeps in, followed, at a more sedate pace, by Harry.)

AMY: Daddy!

(She runs to Arthur and hugs him.)

ARTHUR: My baby girl! I knew you must be here.
How was the airplane? Packed this time of year?

AMY: Horrible. Lucky Nancy and Harry picked me up or I'd
still be at that awful airport.

ARTHUR: Then thank you, Harry, for that extra trip.
Now where's my other daughter? Pip, pip, pip!

NANCY: *(Entering:)* Here I am. I was just neatening up a little.
Honestly, Daddy, "pip, pip, pip"? Even for you that's terrible.

(She hugs Arthur.)

ARTHUR: Well, now our little party all have come.
Your elder brother and his latest one...
I can't keep track...Virginia! That's the dame...
Arrived a little while before you came.

NANCY: Yeah, I saw them going up. When's dinner?

ARTHUR: As soon as Gloria will let the maid
Get on with cooking it. You'd think she paid
The woman's salary, the way she takes
Up all the poor girl's time, for goodness sake!

NANCY: *(Rolling her eyes:)* Knowing Aunt Gloria, she's
probably making Collette re-make the bed, re-dust the room,
and re-arrange the furniture. I'll go see if I can pry the poor
thing loose. Gloria likes me—well, more than she likes most
people, anyway.

(She exits, followed by Harry. Amy takes Arthur's arm.)

AMY: Come on, Daddy. Let's check out the kitchen. We may
not be able to cook like Collette, but between us we ought to
be able to figure out the coffee maker. Boy could I use a cup.

(They exit to the kitchen. Lights fade to black. Music may be

used to indicate the passage of time. Suddenly, in the dark, several loud explosions, like blasting or fireworks, followed almost immediately by the sound of a violent avalanche.)

(Pause.)

(A flashlight beam pierces the darkness, followed by Mark, carrying a flashlight and entering from the bedrooms. He is dressed in boxer shorts and a hastily tied bathrobe — though it's hard to tell in the dark. It is the middle of the night and black as pitch outside.)

MARK: Everyone all right?

(Artie enters, carrying a lighted candle. He wears a handsome two-piece pajama set.)

ARTIE: Evidently the power's out. What was it—an avalanche?

MARK: Darned if I know. Sounded like it.

(Arthur enters in pajamas and a sumptuous robe. He's the first to have bothered with slippers — bunny ones. He carries a battery-powered lantern. Muriel is right behind him swaddled in a robe, also wearing slippers, though more conventional ones.)

ARTHUR: Is anybody hurt? We heard a sound
As if some foul disaster shook the ground.

MARK: Nobody knows, Dad.

MURIEL: Surely not—they've all been asleep. After such a big meal, so late in the evening, I didn't think anything could wake me. Collette really outdid herself cooking. You know, for someone who grew up as a magician's assistant in a traveling carnival, she really does cook like a dream.

ARTIE: Evidently the power's out.

(During the following conversation, the rest of the family, except Virginia and Collette, drift on. All are dressed for bed in one way

or another. Each carries some kind of inadequate light source, except Gloria.)

MARK: You said that already.

ARTIE: Yes, and it's still true.

MURIEL: There's a generator, I think.

MARK: If there's any gas. I'll go.

(He exits towards the front entrance.)

GLORIA: There was no flashlight in my room. Why was there no flashlight in my room?

MARY: Was there a bomb?

GLORIA: I had to grope my way like a blind person.

MURIEL: *(To Mary:)* No, dear, I expect it was an avalanche.

ANTHONY: Cool!

MARK: *(Off, from entryway:)* I can't see a blessed thing in here! Whosever boots these are, I'm borrowing them! And I think this is Artie's parka! It's snowing like you wouldn't believe! Wish me luck!

(We hear the door open, the sound of a storm, and the door slamming.)

ARTIE: He <u>would</u> take mine. He'd better not get it dirty.

GLORIA: It's shoddy housekeeping. Where is that maid? Collette!

MURIEL: Now, Gloria, no one can think of everything. Collette is doing a great job, all in all.

ANTHONY: Anyway, how was she supposed to know there'd be an avalanche?

GLORIA: Well! In my day, young children did not speak up to their elders!

HARRY: Come to think of it, though, where is Collette? Time like this, you'd expect her to be fluttering around being all French.

(The phone rings — two short rings, pause, two short rings, pause, etc.)

AMY: Well, at least we know the phone works.

ARTHUR: Good heavens, what a time for that to ring!
And where's the phone? I cannot see a thing!

(He tries to look for it with his battery lantern, but it's not very directional.)

MURIEL: It's in the corner.

(Someone with a better flashlight helpfully illuminates the phone and Arthur moves to it and picks it up.)

ARTHUR: *(On phone:)* Hello! Hello! It's Arthur Hopkins here.
It's very late, not a good time, I fear.

(He listens, a stunned look on his face. Several of the others notice and look at him.)

NANCY: Well, who is it?

ARTHUR: *(Staring at the phone, still in his hand:)* How very odd — and also not polite.
To call with such a message late at night!

ARTIE: Who is it?

ARTHUR: I've no idea. They just said, "That's one down."
And then they hung up — slammed the phone right down.

ARTIE: "That's one down"? What on earth does that mean?

ARTHUR: They just said, "That's one down," and nothing more.
I don't know what it means. I'll think it o'er.

(He hangs up the phone. There is a loud click, and the lights

come up. The cast is revealed in tableau, scattered around the living room. Center stage, Collette's body lies.)

(Note: Obviously, before this point it is important that nobody shine a light that reveals Collette's body prematurely.)

AMY: About time!

ARTIE: Oh, good, the generator's kicked in. Good grief! Collette's fainted!

(Muriel kneels by Collette and shakes her by the shoulder.)

MURIEL: Wake up, Collette, dear! What's the matter with you?

AMY: Somebody get her a glass of water.

HARRY: Or brandy, if there is any. I'll go.

(He exits to the kitchen.)

NANCY: Somebody ought to get a blanket or something.

ANTHONY: I'll go.

(He exits to the bedrooms. As he goes, he passes Virginia, fully dressed, as she enters from the bedrooms.)

MURIEL: Collette! Collette! *(To the others:)* She's really out.

GLORIA: Slap her face.

VIRGINIA: What on earth is going on? How anyone can sleep...

MURIEL: I <u>will</u> <u>not</u> slap her face! Collette! *(To the others:)* I think there's something really wrong with her!

(Nancy kneels to help Muriel revive Collette.)

ARTHUR: *(Musing:)* "One down..."? "One down..."? That's all they said. "One down..."?

(He ponders, a stunned look on his face. Several of the others

notice and look at him.)

NANCY: I can't find a pulse!

(Harry enters from the kitchen with a glass of water.)

HARRY: Couldn't find any brandy, but here's a glass of water.

AMY: That's all they said? "That's one down"? What could that mean?

HARRY: I can't imagine.

NANCY: *(Grimly:)* Well, I think I can.

HARRY: What?

NANCY: I think she's dead. I can't find a pulse. And she's not breathing.

ARTIE: Oh, nonsense. You're just not doing it right. Let me!

(He kneels by the body to try for a pulse as Anthony enters from the bedrooms with a blanket or comforter. We hear the sound of the outside door opening and closing from the entrance hall.)

ANTHONY: I found a blanket.

VIRGINIA: Is that from our bed?

NANCY: Since when do you know how to do it any better than I do? Here, Harry, give me that water.

(He hands her the water and she dashes it in Collette's face. Mark enters from the front hallway, still wearing boots [pink] and a parka.)

MARK: I got the generator started, but there's not a whole lot of gas left.

VIRGINIA: Those are my boots!

ARTIE: Good grief! I think she's dead!

NANCY: Of course she is!

MARK: Who's dead?

ANTHONY: Are you sure?

NANCY: She's not breathing and there's no pulse. And she's cold as ice.

GLORIA: Dead?

(Very slowly, Gloria turns to look at the body. She takes a deep breath and screams. Then she collapses in a heap.)

ARTHUR: *(Irritated right out of his verse:)* Oh, for heaven's sake!

MURIEL: Gloria!

(Muriel rushes to Gloria's side.)

VIRGINIA: Dead? How could she be dead?

MURIEL: She's fainted!

ARTIE: *(Snapping, know-it-all:)* She hasn't fainted, she's dead!

MURIEL: Gloria has fainted. Help me get her on the couch. Bring that blanket.

(Mary and Anthony help Muriel to drag/carry the prone Gloria onto a couch. Muriel fans her face.)

MARY: Wake up, Great-Aunt Gloria!

MURIEL: Where are her smelling salts?

ARTHUR: Please don't mind Gloria — she faints all the time. Collette is dead — she's been here all the time.

(He kneels by Collette's body and confirms what everyone has been saying. Meanwhile, Muriel is still concerned with Gloria.)

MURIEL: Ask Collette. She'll know where they are. *(Realizing:)* Oh.

HARRY: Someone call the police!

(Mark picks up the phone, jiggles the cradle a few time, and puts

it down.)

MARK: The phone's dead.

AMY: What do you mean?

MARK: Dead, as in doesn't work. No dial tone.

HARRY: But it just rang!

MARK: Well, it's dead now.

ARTIE: Nonsense.

(He storms across and grabs the phone.)

MURIEL: She's coming around.

BETSY: Coming around? I thought she was dead!

ARTIE: Very strange. The phone's dead.

MARK: *(Dryly:)* Don't mind me.

BETSY: What are we going to do?

GLORIA: Stop waving your hand in my face, Muriel! You're not the Queen! What am I doing in this davenport?

HARRY: Somebody's back in form.

MURIEL: You fainted, dear.

GLORIA: Nonsense! I never faint.

ARTHUR: The phone is dead — the line's down, I suppose. *(An idea:)* A cell phone! Anyone got one of those?

ARTIE: Of course not! You told us not to bring them. <u>Ordered</u> us, really.

VIRGINIA: That's right. It was right there in the invitations: "Everyone will please remember,/Each and every family member,/When you pack your boots and jackets,/Leave behind your phones and gadgets."

ARTHUR: I don't remember, but it well may be.
I might have thought it would be nice, you see,
For people to engage in pleasant chats
Instead of simply staring at their laps.
But still, it was an inconvenient day
To suddenly start doing what I say.

GLORIA: What time is it? Why is it dark outside?

HARRY: Yes, well, if we can't contact the authorities, we can't. In any case, we can't leave poor Collette lying on the living room floor, can we?

MURIEL: I suppose not. We'd better put her in her own room.

MARK: Better open all the windows in there and shut off the radiator—there's no telling how long she'll be there, and we don't want her getting ripe.

MURIEL: Honestly, Mark, what a way to put it! And in front of the children!

ANTHONY: Oh, we don't mind.

MARY: We hear worse on T.V.

GLORIA: What is everyone talking about?

BETSY: What do you mean, there's no telling? Can't someone take a car out in the morning and bring help?

MARK: Not hardly. You don't seem to understand how it is up here. If that was an avalanche—and I'm pretty sure it was—there could be forty feet of snow blocking the pass.

NANCY: Nobody's getting through there until spring.

BETSY: *(Really alarmed:)* Spring! But that's months from now!

NANCY: Welcome to the mountains.

BETSY: But...I can't...

ARTHUR: Now, don't you panic. There's no need to swoon. Someone will notice that we're missing soon.

NANCY: Sure. That's what happened the last time. They sent a helicopter.

BETSY: The last time? *(To Mark:)* You mean this has happened before?

MARK: Sure...well, not the dead girl part, but yeah, there was an avalanche five years ago. That's how come I recognize the sound.

ANTHONY: But it wasn't quite the same sound!

MARY: How do you know? You were six!

BETSY: If it's happened before, you'd think somebody might have mentioned it when he invited me to this place.

ANTHONY: I remember. Last time there was the same thundering and booming, but this time, before that was a really big bang. Like a bomb.

ARTIE: Nonsense. You're letting your imagination run away with you.

VIRGINIA: As usual. Though calling it imagination instead of making up stories is...

ANTHONY: I'm not making up stories!

MARY: You know, it sounded like that to me, too.

BETSY: I can't believe you trapped me up here for goodness-knows-how-long!

ARTIE: Anthony, don't shout at your mother!

MARY: She's not our mother!

ARTIE: Well, don't shout at her anyway!

GLORIA: Why is everyone shouting?!

(Mark puts two fingers in his mouth and emits a shrill whistle. [Note: if the actor can't do this, find some other way to make an arresting sound – maybe a brass bell is lying around or something.])

MARK: Um...sorry, but...um...dead body? Can we maybe...

MURIEL: Of course. Harry, could you help Mark carry her? Anthony, run along ahead and open the door to her room. Be sure to lock it when you're done.

ARTIE: Why?

MURIEL: We don't want *(Glancing meaningfully at Mary and Anthony:)* anyone going in there by mistake. Meanwhile, I suggest the rest of us go back to bed.

VIRGINIA: But—

MURIEL: There's nothing we can do about anything just now. We'll think more in the morning.

(Mark and Harry pick up Collette's body and begin to carry it towards the bedrooms.)

GLORIA: What are they doing? Is Collette...is she <u>dead</u>? Oh, my gracious!

(She takes a deep breath and screams. Then she collapses in a heap.)

ARTHUR: Oh, for crying out loud!

(Blackout. Music may be used to indicate the passage of time.)

(Lights up on the family [except Collette] gathered in the living room. Some may be seated on various chairs, couches, or whatever, while some stand or lean. Mary and Anthony sit on the floor. It is morning.)

NANCY: But how did she die?

AMY: I have no idea.

ARTIE: Mark's the scientist.

MARK: I'm a <u>physicist</u>. Or will be when I graduate.

NANCY: <u>If</u> he graduates.

MARK: What do I know about dead bodies?

HARRY: But shouldn't somebody examine her?

ARTIE: Like who? Whom?

NANCY: No, you were right the first time.

ARTHUR: Grammar aside, I disagree completely.
Her body is reposing very sweetly.
So why should we disturb her final rest?
Leave her alone. I think it would be best.

HARRY: But if she was murdered...

ARTIE: But we don't <u>know</u> that. She may have died of natural causes...

MURIEL: At her age? She was healthy as a horse.

ARTIE: And we've no business interfering with her in any case!

MARY: But that phone call! "That's one down"!

ANTHONY: *(Agreeing:)* <u>Obviously</u> she was murdered!

VIRGINIA: Shut up, you two. The grown-ups are talking.

ARTIE: Anyway, Mark just said he wouldn't know what to look for. I doubt any of us could do any better.

MURIEL: He's right. Maybe we should leave it to the authorities.

BETSY: But the authorities aren't <u>here</u>! And how are we going to call them?

(Nancy picks up the phone.)

NANCY: The phone's still dead.

HARRY: There must be some way we can get a signal out. Light a fire or something.

MARY: *(Suddenly struck by an idea:)* Hey, I have an idea!

ARTIE: *(To Mary:)* Sweetheart, the grown-ups are talking. *(To Harry:)* What kind of fire? Where?

HARRY: I don't know. The yard?

MARK: There's four feet of snow out there. And what are you going to burn?

MARY: But listen! Remember the Fourth of July?

VIRGINIA: Mary, stop interrupting. Honestly, Artie, I don't know why you couldn't have taught your children better manners.

ANTHONY: *(Catching on:)* Hey, yeah! I know what your idea is, sis! Hey, everybody...

(The adults look at Anthony.)

ARTIE: Anthony, please!

HARRY: Well, okay, then the roof.

NANCY: You'd burn the place to the ground, dear. I know it's huge, but it's still a cabin. Made of logs. That burn.

AMY: Besides, somebody's bound to get worried about us soon. They'll send a search party.

ARTHUR: Well, there you go, then. We'll just have to wait 'til someone does. Meanwhile, it's time to eat.
I move we all adjourn to break our fast.
Upon some wholesome early morn repast.

MARK: I'll second that. To the kitchen, ho!

BETSY: How can you think of eating? There's a dead woman in the house.

MARK: Well, our going hungry isn't going to bring her back. Come on.

(All the adults exit towards the kitchen. Mary and Anthony exchange looks.)

ANTHONY: I don't care what they say. Obviously Collette was murdered.

MARY: And obviously the murderer is whoever made that phone call. Seriously — "That's one down"? What do they need, a map?

ANTHONY: But who was it? And how did they get away?

MARY: I don't know. Snowmobile, maybe?

ANTHONY: *(Suddenly excited:)* We could look for tracks!

MARY: What?

ANTHONY: Outside. Maybe the murderer left tracks!

MARY: Silly. That's for the detectives.

ANTHONY: What detectives? We can't call any detectives. And if we could, they couldn't get here.

MARY: So?

ANTHONY: So maybe <u>we</u> can be the detectives!

(The adults begin to drift back from the kitchen in poor spirits.)

MARK: Well, that was disappointing.

MURIEL: I completely forgot Collette wasn't here to cook breakfast.

AMY: Not even any coffee ready! I'd kill for some coffee.

HARRY: Better not say that, in the circumstances.

BETSY: How can you joke?

GLORIA: I demand my tea! I'm an old woman!

ANTHONY: Isn't there really any food at all?

MARK: Oh, there's plenty of food. The freezer's full of food. So's the pantry. Just not cooked.

ARTIE: Well, then we'll have to cook it ourselves. Nancy, Virginia, er...Miss Macy, go on in there and make bacon and eggs or something.

BETSY: Why us? Because we're women?

VIRGINIA: What on earth makes you think I know how to cook?

BETSY: I'm a waitress, not a cook.

ARTIE: You mean to say none of you can cook?

BETSY: I can cook. Of course I can cook...

MARK: Um, sweety—being able to boil water without burning it does not equal "can cook."

BETSY: But I'm not going to. Not just because I'm a woman, I'm not.

HARRY: I can make instant coffee—only there isn't any. And I'm darned if I can figure out that space age coffeemaker in there.

VIRGINIA: So we all starve, then?

MARY: You know, I'll bet Anthony and I can figure something out.

ANTHONY: Sure. We all have to take home-ec at school.

VIRGINIA: Will you kids quit butting in?

MARK: Now wait a minute, Ginny—

VIRGINIA: Do. NOT. Call. Me. GINNY!

MARK: Sorry—so sorry! Virginia. If the kids say they can cook, why not let 'em? I'm starving here!

GLORIA: I want my tea!

VIRGINIA: Mark, my dear, you don't have to live with these hoydens. Of course they <u>say</u> they can cook. They <u>say</u> they can keep their rooms clean, too. But what they <u>say</u> and what they <u>do</u>...

ARTIE: Mark's right, Virginia. If they make a mess of things, we're no worse off than we are now, after all.

MURIEL: *(Kindly:)* And I'm sure they won't. Come on, you two. I'll help.

MARY: Thank you! *(To others, haughtily:)* Breakfast will be served in twenty minutes.

(Mary, Anthony and Muriel exit towards the kitchen.)

VIRGINIA: Well, then I'm going back to bed.

(She exits towards the bedrooms.)

HARRY: *(To Mark:)* You'd better show me where that generator is.

MARK: Come on.

(They exit towards the front entrance.)

NANCY: *(To Artie:)* Come on, brother mine. Let's go see if there's any wood in the box room. If we're stuck here, we may as well have a fire.

(They exit towards the kitchen.)

GLORIA: I would like to lie down.

ARTHUR: Yes, Gloria. Just come along with me.
I'll help you up to bed, just wait and see.

(He takes her arm and leads her off toward the bedrooms.

Blackout. Music may play to indicate the passage of time.)

(Lights up on the living room. It is early afternoon. If possible, a fire burns in the fireplace. Mary and Anthony are alone.)

ANTHONY: Who knew grown-ups could be so helpless?

MARY: Hey, at least Uncle Mark figured out the coffeemaker.

ANTHONY: Feeding all these people is a lot of work. How are we going to get time to detect?

MARY: I know. Poor Collette. I never realized how hard she used to work. I'm sorry she's dead. She was sort of nice.

ANTHONY: That's why we have to find out who killed her. And how they got away.

MARY: I still think that's a job for the cops. We should concentrate on getting them here.

ANTHONY: Well, you had a good idea about that, even if the grown-ups wouldn't listen. Those left-over fireworks from the Fourth of July.

MARY: *(Nodding:)* I'm pretty sure they're stored in the hall closet. We can set them off out the attic window or something.

ANTHONY: We'll have to wait until night-time, or nobody will ever see them.

(The phone rings. Two rings, pause, two rings, pause, etc. Startled, Mary goes to the phone and picks it up. As she listens, Anthony stares. Nancy comes running in from the bedrooms, followed more slowly by Arthur and Muriel.)

MARY: Hello?

(She listens.)

ANTHONY: What is it?

NANCY: I heard the phone!

MARY: *(Holding the phone and staring at it:)* "That's two down."

ARTHUR: What?

MARY: That's what they said. "That's two down."

MURIEL: Are you sure?

MARY: *(Irritated:)* Well, of course I'm sure.

>*(She hangs up the phone. We hear the front door opening, sounds of storm, and the front door slamming.)*

MARK: *(Off:)* Carry him into the living room!

ARTIE: *(Off:)* He's darn heavy!

>*(Mark and Artie stagger in from the front entrance, carrying Harry's body between them.)*

ANTHONY: What happened?

NANCY: Oh, my goodness! Harry!

>*(She rushes to Harry's side as Mark and Artie deposit him on a couch.)*

ANTHONY: What happened?

MARK: We went out to check on the generator and bring in some more firewood from the shed.

ARTIE: It's still snowing like blazes out there.

NANCY: But what happened? Harry, speak to me!

MARK: I'm sorry, sis, but he won't.

NANCY: What are you saying?

ARTIE: As we came up the path, there were Harry's boots, sticking out of a snowdrift.

MARK: With the rest of him attached. Buried head first. We pulled him out as fast as we could, but he was gone.

MURIEL: Gone? You're not saying...

ARTIE: He must have somehow lost his footing and tumbled into the bank. Suffocated, poor devil.

(Nancy has been running her hand through Harry's hair. Suddenly she gives a little gasp.)

NANCY: His head's all bloody!

ARTIE: What?

NANCY: *(Showing a bloody hand:)* Look. His head's all bloody!

ARTIE: Must have hit it on something as he fell.

MARY: "That's two down."

ARTIE: Mary, this is hardly a time for jokes!

MARY: No, that's what they said! On the phone.

(Artie snatches up the phone and listens, rattling the cradle a few times.)

ARTIE: The phone's dead, Mary.

MARY: I don't care! It rang and I answered and they said, "That's two down."

(Artie snorts derisively.)

NANCY: I heard the phone ring too, you know.

MURIEL: Arthur and I did too.

ANTHONY: Somebody murdered Uncle Harry like they did Collette.

ARTIE: Nonsense!

ANTHONY: They hit him over the head and dumped him in the snowbank.

ARTIE: You don't know that. He could have slipped and hit his head on something.

MARK: Like what, Artie? I didn't see anything in that snow but snow. And poor Harry, of course.

MARY: Don't you see, Dad? The phone call proves it! "That's two down"!

ARTIE: The phone is <u>dead</u>!

ARTHUR: Mary, are you sure that's what they said?
And that's the reason our poor Harry's dead?

MARY: Of course I'm sure. I'm not a child. Well, okay, I am a child, but I'm not an idiot!

ARTIE: This is terrible! We've got to find a way to contact the authorities!

ANTHONY: Mary and I thought of a way.

ARTIE: *(To Anthony:)* You stay out of this. *(To the adults:)* There must be some way to send a signal.

ANTHONY: But, listen!

MURIEL: Meanwhile, what do we do with poor Harry?

NANCY: Oh, Harry!

(Gloria enters from the bedrooms.)

GLORIA: What is all this noise? How is a person supposed to enjoy her afternoon nap with all this racket? *(Noticing Anthony and Mary:)* Oh. I might have known it was you two. *(To Artie:)* Honestly, Arthur, Jr., if you must bring children on these little outings, you might at least have the courtesy to —

MURIEL: Not now, Gloria, dear. We've got a situation here.

GLORIA: Situation? What situation? Why is Harry lying there like that? And Nancy, why are your hands all dirty?

MURIEL: Now Gloria, don't worry yourself. Don't look.

GLORIA: Don't look at what? Is that blood? What's wrong with Harry?

MURIEL: Well, dear, I'm very much afraid...

(Pause.)

GLORIA: He's dead, isn't he?

(She takes a deep breath and screams. Then she collapses in a heap.)

ARTHUR: Not again! For crying out loud!

(Anthony exits towards the kitchen.)

MURIEL: Never mind. Mark and Arthur Jr., take poor Harry out to the front porch. He'll be cold enough there to keep. Put him in one of those lounge chairs. Better cover him up with a tarp or something in case the snow blows onto the porch.

NANCY: *(On a sob:)* Oh, Harry!

(Mark and Artie carry Harry's body off towards the front entrance, accompanied by Nancy, who tries to hold Harry's hand as he's carried. Before Muriel can get to Gloria to try and revive her, Anthony returns from the kitchen at a run, and dashes a glass of water in Gloria's face. She sputters to life instantly.)

GLORIA: How dare you!

MURIEL: *(With a reproachful look at Anthony:)* Never mind, dear. You fainted again is all.

GLORIA: I never faint!

MURIEL: Of course you don't. Come along now—let's go to the kitchen and get you a nice cup of tea.

(They exit towards the kitchen with Arthur following, leaving Anthony and Mary alone.)

ANTHONY: Was it a man or woman?

MARY: Who?

ANTHONY: On the phone? "That's two down."

MARY: I couldn't tell. It sounded like they were putting on a funny voice. Sort of in-between. Like it could be a man trying to sound like a woman or a woman trying to sound like a man.

ANTHONY: This is getting serious. I liked Uncle Harry.

MARY: I know. We need to get ready to send our signal.

ANTHONY: I'll get the fireworks box.

(He exits towards the front entrance. He returns momentarily, carrying a large cardboard box.)

MARY: Put them down over here—away from the fire. *(Note: if there is no fireplace, skip the 2nd half of this line.)*

ANTHONY: *(Setting the box down:)* They're not as heavy as I expected.

MARY: Well, you're bigger now.

ANTHONY: *(Opening the box:)* Still. Oh. That's why.

MARY: What's why? Why what?

ANTHONY: *(Staring into the box:)* It's empty.

MARY: It can't be. Maybe you grabbed the wrong box.

ANTHONY: No, it's the right box. There's some firecracker wrappers and stuff in here. But no fireworks.

MARY: But nobody's been here since last summer! I <u>know</u> there were a bunch of them left.

ANTHONY: Well, they're not here now. *(A sudden realization:)* Oh! Oh my gosh!

MARY: You're right!

ANTHONY: I <u>knew</u> I heard an explosion before the avalanche! Somebody set it off on purpose! They stole our fireworks and set them off to trigger the avalanche!

MARY: Somebody <u>wants</u> us all trapped up here!

ANTHONY: So they can murder us one by one! "One down"! "Two down"! Who's next?

MARY: We have to tell the grown-ups!

ANTHONY: Sure. As if they'll believe us. Dad will say we must have used up all the firecrackers last summer.

MARY: But I know we didn't!

ANTHONY: And Virginia will say, "Shut up, children. The grown-ups are talking."

MARY: We still have to tell them. Maybe Uncle Mark will believe us.

ANTHONY: He's out on the front porch. Come on. We can look around for tracks, too. We still don't know how the guy's coming and going.

MARY: Only we'll have to search fast. Don't forget, we have to cook supper. Or go hungry.

ANTHONY: Let's go. *(Calling off:)* Uncle Mark!

(They run off towards the front entrance. Blackout. Music may play to indicate the passage of time.)

(Lights up on the living room. It is evening. The room is empty except for Gloria, who lies in a heap in the middle of the floor. The phone rings. Two rings, pause, two rings, pause, etc. Mark enters from the bedrooms. He doesn't notice Gloria. He goes to the phone and picks it up.)

MARK: Hello?

(He listens. Arthur enters from the kitchen and nearly trips over Gloria.)

ARTHUR: Oh, for the love of Mike!

MARK: *(To phone:)* What do you mean, "That makes three"? What three?

ARTHUR: Gloria, honest to goodness, if you faint one more time, so help me...

(He bends down and shakes her.)

MARK: *(To phone:)* Listen, buster, I don't know who you are, but this isn't funny. Hmm... *(To Arthur:)* They hung up. What are you doing?

ARTHUR: Gloria's out again. Go get some water.
That approach worked last time — nothing better.

MARK: Maybe not this time.

(He bends to get a better look. Mary and Anthony run in from the front entrance.)

MARY: We heard the phone!

ARTHUR: *(Standing up, to Mark:)* What do you mean? She'll wake for sure and then
(Grinning:) She'll yell at us for soaking her again.

(Muriel runs in from the kitchen.)

MARK: The phone. "That makes three." They said, "That makes three."

MURIEL: Gloria!

MARK: Um, Mom...I'm pretty sure she's dead.

MURIEL: Not necessarily. The phone call might have been about something else.

ANTHONY: Who is it this time? Is it Virginia?

MARK: *(To Muriel:)* It's not just the phone call.

ANTHONY: Great Aunt Gloria?

ARTHUR: What do you mean, not just the phone call?

MARK: It's also this great big honking knife in her back.

MURIEL: What? *(To Mary and Anthony:)* Don't look!

(Mary and Anthony look where Mark is looking.)

MARY: Too late.

ANTHONY: That is a big honking knife!

MURIEL: This has got to stop! Children, move away. Mark, help your father carry her out to the porch. We'll put her with Harry. What else can we do? There must be another tarp in the box room.

(They carry her awkwardly between them and exit towards the front entrance, leaving Mary and Anthony alone.)

ANTHONY: What are we going to do? They're dropping like flies. How is the guy doing it?

MARY: I don't know. It's like a stupid murder mystery or something. Especially those phone calls—when the phone doesn't even work.

ANTHONY: I know. I'm going to be hearing them in my sleep. Ring, ring! Ring, ring!

MARY: I hear you.

ANTHONY: Ring, ring! Ring, ring!

MARY: I get it.

ANTHONY: Ring, ring! Ring, ring!

MARY: Stop it! Wait a minute. Do that again.

ANTHONY: You want me to stop or do it again?

MARY: Do it again, just the same way.

ANTHONY: Ring, ring!

MARY: That's it!

ANTHONY: *(Indignantly:)* You told me to do it again!

MARY: No, I mean, that's it! That's how he's doing it!

ANTHONY: What is?

MARY: That's just how the phone rang, isn't it? Every time?

ANTHONY: How what?

MARY: "Ring, ring! Ring, ring! Ring, ring!"

ANTHONY: So?

MARY: Not "Ring! Ring! Ring!"

ANTHONY: So?

MARY: So since when is that how the phone rings? It goes "Ring! Ring! Ring!"

ANTHONY: Hey, yeah!

MARY: Not "Ring, ring! Ring, ring! Ring, ring!" <u>That's</u> the <u>intercom</u>!

ANTHONY: The interwho?

MARY: The intercom! You know — so people can call other people in the house! Don't you remember? Grandma used to use it to call folks for dinner! Or to call Collette if she needed something. It rings differently so folks will know what it is!

ANTHONY: I remember now! You dial 99 or something, and it rings another phone in the house.

MARY: That's how he's doing it! He's calling on the intercom!

ANTHONY: But if the phone doesn't work...

MARY: Don't you see? The phones don't work because the wires are down outside. From the avalanche.

ANTHONY: Which we know the guy set off on purpose with fireworks, even if no one believes us.

MARY: But there wasn't any avalanche <u>inside</u> the house! I bet the intercom still works fine.

ANTHONY: One way to find out.

(He goes to the phone, picks it up and dials. After a moment, we hear it ring. Two rings, pause, two rings, pause.)

MARY: I knew it!

(Just as Anthony hangs up the phone, we hear:)

MURIEL: *(Off:)* Hello?

ANTHONY: You know what this means, don't you?

MURIEL: *(Off:)* Hello? That's strange.

MARY: Yep.

MURIEL: *(Off:)* There's no one there.

MARY & ANTHONY: *(Unison:)* The calls are coming from inside the house!

(Blackout. In the dark we hear:)

MURIEL: *(Off:)* They must have hung up. And the phone still doesn't work!

(Music may play to indicate the passage of time.)

(Lights up on the living room. It is mid-morning. A family conference is taking place. Arthur holds the floor, surrounded by Muriel, Artie, Virginia, Mark, Betsy, Amy, Mary and Anthony.)

ARTHUR: I've asked you all to come together now
To see if we can possibly learn how
Some unmentionable cad has got away
With murdering three people in this way.
This business has gone far enough, I'd say.
I'm sure you all agree with me today.

ARTIE: More than far enough.

ARTHUR: Since we've been here, three souls have passed away.
It's got to stop. It's got to stop, I say!

NANCY: But how?

ARTHUR: My grandchildren are smart, without a doubt.
Because of what these two have figured out,
We now assume this unspeakable louse
Is hiding somewhere here inside this house.

ARTIE: *(Sarcastic:)* That's comforting.

ARTHUR: *(Pointedly ignoring him:)* So what we're going to do
is search the house
From top to bottom. Not even a mouse
Must pass our notice. Also search outside
In case there is a place for him to hide.

BETSY: How do you know it's a he?

VIRGINIA: *(Snorting:)* Oh, please!

ARTHUR: *(Bowing:)* I stand corrected. He might be a she.
Now, I'll need volunteers — who will it be?

MARK: Wait a minute. Shouldn't we stay in pairs?

ARTIE: Why?

MARK: Er...I don't know. That's what they always do in books. For safety, I guess.

MURIEL: *(Taking over:)* Fine. We'll search in pairs. Ginny and I will do the bedrooms.

VIRGINIA: Do. NOT. Call. Me. Ginny!

MURIEL: Virginia and I will do the bedrooms. They all have keys in the doors. After we search one, we'll lock the door and take the key with us.

BETSY: Why?

AMY: How are we going to get back into our rooms?

MURIEL: You can have them back when the search is done. This way, the miscreant will not be able to double back and hide in a room we've already searched.

BETSY: Oh. Good thinking.

ARTHUR: Be sure and search the bedrooms one and all.
The bathrooms too — and look in every stall.

VIRGINIA: <u>All</u> the bedrooms? Even Collette's? I'm not going in there with a stiff.

MARK: Ha! Probably getting pretty ripe, too.

MURIEL: *(Wincing at his choice of words:)* That won't be necessary. Her door has been locked since we carried her up there and there are only two keys. One is right here. *(Pulling a key from her pocket:)* And the other is on a chain around poor Collette's neck.

MARK: I'll do the outdoor stuff. I'll take Anthony with me.

ANTHONY: Sure thing, Uncle Mark.

MURIEL: Fine. Amy, why don't you and Miss Macy take the kitchen, along with the pantries and the root cellar?

BETSY: Kitchen. Figures.

AMY: Oh, let's just get on with it!

BETSY: Well, excuse me! I'm just saying.

AMY: Well, don't.

ARTHUR: And young Mary and I will take the attic.
(Winking at Mary:) A spooky job for us. You think you'll panic?

MARY: Can't be any spookier than Anthony's room on laundry day.

ANTHONY: Hey! I resemble that remark!

MURIEL: Good, good. Now, if everyone understands their jobs, let's get searching. This murderer has to be hiding somewhere. Let's find him.

(All disperse in the various directions indicated. Blackout. Music may play to indicate the passage of time.)

(Lights up on the living room, later the same afternoon. Nancy, Mark, Betsy, Amy, Mary and Anthony are deep in discussion.)

NANCY: I can't understand it. We searched everywhere. There's nobody here.

AMY: Maybe whoever it was went away.

BETSY: Wouldn't that be nice? Or else he found a hiding place we didn't.

NANCY: But our family has owned this place for years—we know all the hiding places! I just don't get it.

MARY: Um...excuse me, but...duh!

ANTHONY: Yeah, duh!

MARK: What duh?

ANTHONY: It's so obvious!

MARY: I don't know why we didn't see it ages ago. Doesn't anybody read detective stories anymore?

NANCY: What's obvious?

MARY: I mean, come on—think about it. The killer has to be in the house, right?

NANCY: We certainly thought so.

MARY: And we searched everywhere, right? And didn't find any strangers hiding in the woodwork?

MARK: So?

ANTHONY: So it's obvious.

MARY & ANTHONY: *(Unison:)* The killer is one of us!

MARY: Has to be!

(Pause, while they all stare at Mary and Anthony.)

NANCY: One of us?

AMY: But that's impossible!

MARY: It's not impossible, it's logical. Look. One: the killer is in the house. Two: there's nobody in the house but us. Three: ipso facto, the killer is one of us!

AMY: But that's terrible!

BETSY: Ipso what?

NANCY: You're saying one of our family killed three people?

ANTHONY: Or Betsy. *(To Betsy:)* No offense. You're like, honorary family now anyway.

BETSY: None taken. Only it's not me. How could it be me? I've only just met everyone.

MARK: *(Kidding:)* Yeah, but how do we know that's really true? Maybe you're a long-lost heir in disguise.

AMY: Given the way you two were kissing yesterday in the shed when you thought no one was looking, that would be pretty sick. Seriously, though, I think it's Virginia.

MARK: Virginia! That actually makes sense. *(To Mary and Anthony:)* Sorry, guys — I know she's your mother.

MARY: She is <u>not</u> our mother! And it might be her.

BETSY: Ooh, I bet it is. She's got a mean mouth.

ANTHONY: And she's a gold-digger.

MARK: Hey, hey — where'd you hear that word?

ANTHONY: From you, Uncle Mark. When you didn't know I

was listening.

NANCY: But that doesn't make any sense! Why would she do it?

BETSY: Well, they do say, out of the mouths of babes...

NANCY: But if she was after Artie's money—or Dad's—wouldn't she kill them first?

BETSY: Practice?

NANCY: Besides, if I know my big brother, there's got to be a pre-nup. She can't possibly inherit. She'd have to be crazy.

AMY: So maybe she <u>is</u> crazy.

NANCY: You just don't want it to be anyone else.

AMY: Well, yeah—do you?

NANCY: I don't want it to be <u>any</u> of us! The freak killed my husband, don't forget. But this is all just speculation. Who we like or don't like doesn't matter. We need evidence!

MARK: We need the cops. How long is it going to take for somebody to figure out we're up here?

(The lights flicker.)

BETSY: What was that?

MARK: Uh oh. The generator must be running low on gas. I think there's one more container left. I'll go fix it.

BETSY: I'm coming with you. *(Kidding:)* In case one of these guys is the killer.

(They exit towards the front entrance.)

AMY: Come on, sis. Let's get some coffee or something.

NANCY: I think I saw some of those cupcakes these two made in the kitchen.

AMY: Cupcakes! Get behind me, temptress! Model—
remember?

NANCY: Coffee it is.

*(They exit towards the kitchen. Mary and Anthony look at each
other. Pause.)*

ANTHONY: Wow.

(Pause.)

You think it really is Virginia?

MARY: Well, actually, yeah, I do. But not because she's a gold-
digger. Seriously, Anthony, do you even know what that
means?

ANTHONY: Sure. It means she's after Dad for his money. But
I don't know if that's true.

MARY: Well, it's not why I suspect her, anyway. But I've been
thinking.

ANTHONY: Never a good sign.

MARY: Shut up! Anyway, it has to be the killer making those
phone calls, right?

ANTHONY: Probably. Unless there's two of them.

MARY: *(Momentarily flummoxed:)* I didn't think of that. But
let's say there's just one killer.

ANTHONY: Fine with me.

MARY: So if the killer is making the phone call, then it has to
be someone who was not in the living room when someone
answered the phone. He had to be on some other extension.

ANTHONY: Hey, yeah, that's true!

MARY: And even if there's one person doing the killing and a
different person doing the calling, at least THAT person can't

have been in the living room when the calls came in.

ANTHONY: So, who was there when they came?

MARY: That's what I'm trying to remember. Okay, the first call.

ANTHONY: "That's one down."

MARY: Exactly. I think everyone was in the living room except Virginia. I remember she wasn't because she came in afterwards, and she was the only person wearing regular clothes instead of PJs. That's suspicious in itself, by the way. Why was she wearing her clothes, unless she was up doing something?

ANTHONY: No, that's just Virginia. She'd never appear in public in her PJs.

MARY: Okay, but it still shows that she could have made that phone call. Oh, and Uncle Mark wasn't there either — he went out to fix the generator. But he could have made the call on the way.

ANTHONY: It's not Uncle Mark! Uncle Mark is nice!

MARY: I like him too, but it's like Aunt Nancy said. We can't go by who we like. We have to go by the evidence. And the evidence says Uncle Mark could have made that call. And Anthony, he could have made the second one, too.

ANTHONY: I don't believe it.

MARY: Remember, it was just you and me in here when that call came. Aunt Nancy and Grandma and Gramps came in right after, so it probably wasn't them, but it could have been Uncle Mark, or Virginia, or Dad, or Great Aunt Gloria — except we know Gloria's not the killer because she was the next victim.

ANTHONY: Gee, I hope it's not Dad. But it's not Uncle Mark.

MARY: It can't be Dad because he was there for the first call. So were Grandma and Gramps.

ANTHONY: It's not Uncle Mark!

MARY: No, I don't think so either—because of the third call. Uncle Mark <u>answered</u> that one. So that leaves just Virginia. She's the only person who wasn't there for any of the three calls.

ANTHONY: Wow. My stepmother is a murderer.

(Artie enters from the bedrooms.)

ARTIE: Oh, there you are, kids. Have you seen your mother?

MARY: She's <u>not</u> our mother.

ANTHONY: No! She's a mur-umph!

(Mary claps her hand over Anthony's mouth. She looks him in the eye and shakes her head.)

ARTIE: What's that?

ANTHONY: Nothing. We haven't seen her.

(Amy and Nancy enter from the kitchen. Amy has a coffee cup in her hand and Nancy is finishing off a cupcake.)

NANCY: *(A little muffled from the cupcake:)* Seen who? Whom?

ARTIE: I was looking for Virginia.

AMY: I thought she was in your room taking a nap.

(The phone rings. Two rings, pause, two rings, pause, etc.)

NANCY: Oh, no!

(They all stare at the phone, but nobody makes a move to answer it. It continues to ring.)

AMY: Well, isn't someone going to get that?

(Arthur and Muriel rush in from the bedrooms. They stop short,

surprised to see everyone not answering the phone. Finally, Muriel breaks the spell.)

MURIEL: Oh, for goodness sake! *(Answering phone:)* Hello?

(She listens, as everyone stares at her. She puts the receiver in the cradle. Pause.)

ARTHUR: *(Prodding:)* Muriel...

MURIEL: *(Voice of despair:)* "That's four."

(Everyone just stares. Into this tableau, Mark and Betsy enter from the front entrance.)

MARK: Well, that takes care of that. She should run for a while now, but we're down to our last tank. Hey, whose idea was it to move Collette down to the porch with the others?

MURIEL: What? What are you talking about? Collette is still locked in her room.

MARK: Then who is that out there? There's three bodies in those lounge chairs, covered with tarps. Harry, Gloria and...who?

(Everyone stares at one another for a long moment. Then they all rush out towards the front entrance in a clump. Blackout. Music may play to indicate the passage of time.)

(Lights up on the living room. It is only a few minutes later. Arthur, Muriel, Artie, Mark, Betsy, Amy, Mary and Anthony enter from the front entrance, all looking shell-shocked.)

ARTHUR: We may as well just leave her where she lies.
Best place for her. It's cold and there's no flies.
An awful way to die, I have to say,
Strangled with expensive lingerie!

MARK: Her own. The very best silk, naturally.

ARTIE: I loved her, you know.

(Pause.)

I mean, I know everyone thinks she married me for my money...and maybe she did. But I loved her.

(Mary, rather awkwardly, puts her arms around her father.)

MURIEL: We know you did, Arthur, Jr. We can't pretend we all liked her very much, but we all feel terrible for you.

ARTIE: *(Meaningly:)* All but one, you mean.

NANCY: *(Exploding in frustration:)* Darn it, who is <u>doing</u> this?

BETSY: *(Dryly:)* Well, not Virginia, anyway.

ARTIE: *(Snapping:)* Of course it wasn't Virginia!

MARY: But...nothing.

AMY: I've got a more interesting question. Who's next?

BETSY: Me.

MURIEL: *(To Amy:)* What a terrible thing to ask!

NANCY: *(To Betsy:)* What? Why?

AMY: *(To Muriel:)* Well, but seriously...

BETSY: Isn't it obvious?

NANCY: Not to me.

BETSY: What do the four dead people have in common?

MARK: Honey, what are you saying?

BETSY: They're not really members of the family!

MURIEL: But my sister —

NANCY: But my husband —

BETSY: Not <u>really</u>. The maid. The annoying old-maid hanger-on. And two in-laws!

ARTIE: So?

BETSY: So obviously somebody is killing off everyone outside the family!

MURIEL: But that's not fair! We all <u>thought</u> of them as...

BETSY: And that makes me next. *(Pregnant pause.)* And it makes one of <u>you</u> the killer!

ARTIE: You have no proof of that at all!

AMY: Wait a minute! All of us have been coming here for years, and nobody ever got murdered before. What's different this time?

BETSY: Now hold on!

AMY: *(To Betsy:)* What's different is <u>you</u>! You're the only one who's new!

MARK: Hey, back off, sis!

AMY: Isn't it strange how as soon as you show up, people start dropping like flies?

BETSY: Sure. That's exactly what you <u>would</u> say.

ARTIE: Come to think of it, what do we really know about you, Miss Macy?

AMY: If that's even your name...

MARK: That's not fair!

ARTIE: How long has Mark even known you? A few weeks?

MARK: Hey, it's longer than that!

AMY: Anybody who reads the papers or watches the news knows there's money in this family. *(To Mark:)* Hey, bro, how did you meet her, huh?

MARK: I—

AMY: I bet she picked you up in a bar or something, didn't she?

BETSY: But I had no idea who his family was!

AMY: So you <u>say</u>.

MURIEL: Both of you, stop it at once!

BETSY: And if I <u>did</u>, I'd have run away as fast as I could go!

AMY: And we thought <u>Virginia</u> was a gold-digger!

BETSY: If I was after money, why would I kill the maid? Or any of them?

AMY: Well, if it comes to that, why would one of us?

BETSY: Oh, that's easy. How about for publicity?

ARTIE: Why would we want that?

BETSY: She keeps telling us she's not a supermodel — she's just a model.

MARK: Babe, maybe we should just...

BETSY: *(To Amy:)* But I'll bet you'd <u>like</u> to be a supermodel, wouldn't you?

AMY: I don't believe this!

BETSY: What's that saying? "There's no such thing as bad publicity!"

AMY: I don't have to listen to this.

BETSY: "Model in tragic mass murder. <u>Super</u>model's family killed in posh ski lodge."

AMY: I'm going to my room. Before I <u>do</u> become a murderer.

 (She storms off towards the bedrooms.)

MARK: Come on, Betsy. Let's take a walk. The air will do you good.

BETSY: *(Snapping:)* Fine!

(They exit towards the front entrance. Arthur puts his hand on Artie's shoulder.)

ARTHUR: I'm sorry, son. As sorry as can be.
This family seems stalked by tragedy.

ARTIE: I'd like to be alone.

(He exits towards the bedrooms.)

MURIEL: I'll go make some tea. *(Sniffing:)* Tea. It seems so inadequate. But what else can one do?

(She exits towards the kitchen. Arthur follows. Neither seems to even notice Mary and Anthony.)

ANTHONY: What does he mean, about tragedy stalking the family? Besides this, I mean?

MARY: He's probably talking about Uncle Phillip.

ANTHONY: Oh, right. The one nobody talks about. Dad told us about that, that time when he was lecturing us not to swim too far from shore.

MARY: Swept out to sea by a rip current or an undertow or something. I guess he washed up a few days later and a long ways away. And then there's Aunt Tessie, of course.

ANTHONY: That's the one who disappeared in France?

MARY: Yeah. Nobody likes to talk about her, either, but Uncle Mark's mentioned her a few times. Apparently she just vanished one day. The police kept looking for years, but nobody ever found her. Everyone figures she's dead, like Uncle Phillip.

ANTHONY: And now like Aunt Virginia and Uncle Harry and Collette and Great Aunt Gloria. I guess that is a fair amount of tragedy for one family.

MARY: Plus, one of them is a killer.

ANTHONY: That, too. But who?

MARY: Well, I hate to say it...

ANTHONY: *(Heatedly:)* So <u>don't</u>! It's not Uncle Mark!

MARY: But Anthony, look at the facts! We thought it was Virginia, but now we know it wasn't. And don't forget, Uncle Mark was missing again when the last phone call came.

ANTHONY: He wasn't <u>missing</u>, he was fixing the generator!

MARY: That's what he <u>says</u>. All we <u>know</u> is that he wasn't here.

ANTHONY: But you said yourself it couldn't be him! He answered the phone himself the last time!

MARY: Yeah, but, look: how do we know what the person actually said?

ANTHONY: You think he faked that phone call? Not Uncle Mark!

MARY: I don't know. Maybe. Nobody was listening in.

ANTHONY: Well, but... *(A sudden realization:)* Wait! He might have pretended to talk on the phone, but he couldn't make it ring! Lots of people heard that!

MARY: Well, I don't know—maybe it was someone else calling, and he just...no, that doesn't work. The outside lines are down. But wait! He was all alone in the living room when the phone rang, right?

ANTHONY: So?

MARY: So why couldn't he have made the call himself, from that same phone, then hung up, picked up the receiver and talked into the dead phone?

ANTHONY: I guess he could. But he didn't. Not Uncle Mark.

MARY: I know what you're saying, Anthony. I do. But if it's not him, it's Aunt Amy. Or Aunt Nancy. Or our own father.

ANTHONY: Aunt Amy thinks it's Betsy.

MARY: But that really doesn't make much sense. Anyway, I like her, too.

ANTHONY: *(Nodding:)* All the ones I didn't like are already dead. I hate to think of someone I like doing something like this.

MARY: Me too.

(Pause.)

ANTHONY: Mary?

MARY: Mmm?

ANTHONY: Do you think Dad really loved her?

MARY: I guess so. He must have.

(Pause.)

ANTHONY: Well, at least if Betsy's right, there's only one more to go.

(The phone rings. Two rings, pause, two rings, pause, etc. They stare at it. Finally, Mary picks it up, just as Arthur and Muriel run on from the kitchen.)

MARY: Hello?

MURIEL: Here, let me have that!

(She tries to take the phone, but Mary holds onto it, listening as all stare. Mark and Betsy enter from the outside entry.)

MARK: We heard the phone!

(Mary hangs up the phone. They all look at her.)

MARY: "Five." That's all they said. "Five."

(Anthony is frantically counting heads to see who's missing. He looks at Mary.)

MARY & ANTHONY: Dad!

(Blackout. Music may play to indicate the passage of time.)

(Lights up on the living room. It is evening. Mary and Anthony are alone.)

ANTHONY: Mary, what are we going to do?

MARY: I guess we go back to Mom's. If anybody ever comes to get us.

ANTHONY: No, I mean about the killer? We have to stop him!

MARY: But how? It's getting faster and faster!

ANTHONY: I can't believe Dad's dead.

MARY: I know. And what a horrible way to die.

ANTHONY: Drowned in his own toilet bowl. Dad would have hated that. He was always such a stinker for dignity.

MARY: I really thought it would be Betsy. Maybe she really is the killer.

ANTHONY: Everybody suspects everybody. We can't even look at each other.

MARY: I know. That was the most silent dinner I ever ate.

ANTHONY: Mary, what if it isn't one of us?

MARY: What? But how could it not be? There's nobody else here.

ANTHONY: Are you sure?

MARY: We searched every room. There's nobody.

ANTHONY: Not every room.

MARY: What? *(A sudden realization:)* Oh my goodness! You're right! But how could there... You're right!

ANTHONY: It has to be. There's nowhere else.

MARY: So now we know how.

ANTHONY: But not who. Or why.

MARY: I think I have an idea about that. It was something Uncle Mark said that got me thinking. If we can just...

AMY: *(Off, shouting:)* You killed my brother.

(Betsy enters from the kitchen.)

BETSY: I didn't kill anyone! Leave me alone!

(Amy pursues her, followed by Mark.)

AMY: All that business about being the next to die! I should have known it was all a bluff.

MARK: Sis, stop it!

AMY: *(Wheeling on him:)* You had to bring her here! A perfect stranger! A waitress, for Pete's sake!

BETSY: *(To Amy:)* What's that supposed to mean? I'm not good enough for this family?

MARK: *(To Betsy:)* Honey, she didn't mean that.

AMY: *(To Mark:)* Don't tell her what I mean!

(Nancy enters from the kitchen.)

BETSY: *(Getting in Amy's face:)* I'm a <u>student</u>, thank you very much! And what are you? A model? That takes a lot of brains!

NANCY: Stop it! Both of you, stop! How is this helping?

BETSY: Oh, what does it matter? We're all going to die anyway! *(Throwing herself into a chair or sofa:)* I wish I never met this family!

(She starts to cry. Mark moves ineffectually to comfort her. Arthur and Muriel enter from the kitchen, looking shell-shocked.)

ARTHUR: Please, everyone! We have to maintain calm,
And stick together, weathering this storm!

(NOTE: Unless one has a very thick New England accent, "calm" does not even remotely rhyme with "storm." However, it is not necessary for Arthur to have a New England accent – he's obviously overwrought. [On the other hand, if the actor happens to be a Boston Brahmin, you can make a joke out of the rhyme.])

NANCY: *(Losing it:)* Calm? How can we be calm? We're trapped here on this stupid mountain with five corpses on the front porch! And one of us is a lunatic!

MURIEL: Arthur's right. We can't start tearing each other apart.

NANCY: One of us already has!

MARY: Maybe not.

(The others suddenly realize Mary and Anthony are present.)

ARTHUR: What?

AMY: Oh, don't start this again!

MARY: It might not be one of us! Anthony and I have an idea!

MURIEL: Now, children, I know you're trying to help...

MARY: Who figured out the phone calls? Why do you treat us like stupid kids?

AMY: Maybe because you <u>are</u> kids?

ANTHONY: But we're not stupid! Why can't you listen to us! We think we know what's going on.

(Betsy suddenly leaps up.)

BETSY: I'm not staying here a minute longer! I'm getting out of here!

MARK: But honey, the snow...

MURIEL: You can't just—

BETSY: I don't care! I'd rather freeze to death out there than sit here waiting to be slaughtered like a pig! *(To Mark:)* You can come with me, or you can stay here to die. I really don't care.

(She storms off towards the front entrance. Mark follows at a run.)

MARK: Wait! Betsy!

(And he's gone.)

ARTHUR: It's all my fault we've come to this sad fate.
I should have listened. Now it is too late.

(He sinks into a chair or sofa and puts his head in his hands. Muriel sits by him and puts her arms around him.)

MURIEL: Don't say that. How could you have known?

ARTHUR: *(Still with head in hands:)* You tried to tell me. Everybody said
It wasn't safe so late. I went ahead.

MURIEL: Arthur, hush.

ARTHUR: Could anyone be such a fool as I,
To invite my entire family to die?

MURIEL: *(To Amy and Nancy:)* Is there any tea? He's about had it.

AMY: I'll get it.

(She exits towards the kitchen.)

NANCY: I'll help.

(She follows.)

MURIEL: *(To Mary and Anthony:)* Children, would you mind leaving us? I think your grandfather and I would like to be alone.

MARY: *(To Anthony:)* Come on. I want to check something. *(To Muriel:)* Grandma, are those old scrapbooks still in the hall closet?

MURIEL: *(Not really paying attention:)* What, dear? Scrapbooks? Why yes, I think so. Why?

MARY: Never mind. Come on, Anthony.

(They exit towards the bedrooms. Muriel and Arthur sit, arms around each other and eyes shut. Slow blackout. Music may play to indicate the passage of time.)

(Lights up on the living room. It is morning. Arthur and Muriel are still seated exactly as we left them, except with empty teacups near them on a little table or something. Amy enters from the kitchen as Nancy enters from the bedrooms. Amy makes a "shhh!" gesture. The following conversation is carried out in whispers.)

AMY: Let them sleep. They've been here all night.

NANCY: The poor dears. They'll be stiff as boots when they wake up.

AMY: It's hard to blame them, though. Poor Daddy must blame himself horribly.

NANCY: At least we can tidy up.

(Tiptoeing so as not to wake her parents, Nancy gathers up the teacups and exits towards the kitchen. Amy follows her out.)

AMY: *(Exiting:)* I'll start the coffee. It's not fair making those kids do all the work.

(Mary and Anthony enter from the bedrooms at a run. They catch sight of Arthur and Muriel and slow to a tiptoeing walk.

Mary carries a large photo album or scrapbook. As they start to cross towards the kitchen, the phone rings. Two rings, pause, two rings, pause, etc. Before either of them can react, Amy rushes in from the kitchen and picks up the phone. She listens as Nancy enters from the kitchen.)

NANCY: Oh my goodness.

(Amy hangs up the phone and stands dumb.)

ANTHONY: What? What did she say?

AMY: "Two for the price of one. That makes six."

NANCY: "Two for the price of one"? What two?

AMY: Omigosh! Mark and Betsy!

MARY: Oh, no!

ANTHONY: Uncle Mark!

AMY: I knew they should never have tried to get out!

NANCY: But if they got stuck in the snow and froze, would that count?

AMY: What do you mean, count?

NANCY: I mean, this guy calls up to take credit for each kill, right? But if it was the elements that did the killing...

AMY: Well, but he drove them out into it, didn't he?

NANCY: *(Shaking her head, bemused:)* Maybe. But there's something else. Wait a minute. Tell me again what they said?

AMY: "Two for the price of one. That makes six."

NANCY: "Six"? Are you sure?

AMY: Yeah—why?

NANCY: Then he made a mistake. Five and two is seven.

MARY: It's not a mistake.

NANCY: Yeah, it is! Collette, Harry, Gloria, Virginia, and Artie is five. Plus Mark and Betsy makes seven.

MARY: No! I mean, yes, it makes seven, but it's not a mistake.

AMY: What?

MARY: Well, actually, it probably was a mistake. But it's not wrong. There are only six.

NANCY: That makes no sense.

ANTHONY: *(Getting it:)* Yes it does! Because we figured out who's doing it!

MARK: *(Off:)* Anybody awake?

(Mark and Betsy enter from the front entrance, still in outdoor gear and very damp and cold.)

AMY: Mark! You're alive!

(She runs to him and hugs him.)

MARK: Barely. Why shouldn't I be?

AMY: There was another phone call. They said "two for the price of one." We thought...

MARK: Great Scott!

AMY: *(Almost triumphant:)* Another mistake! He must have just assumed you'd never make it. He called without making sure!

(Nancy has been staring at Arthur and Muriel.)

NANCY: Um...I don't think it's a mistake.

AMY: Mom! Daddy!

(They rush to Arthur and Muriel, who don't move and clearly never will.)

NANCY: They're ice cold. But what happened?

(Mark rushes over.)

MARK: I don't see a weapon. Or a wound.

BETSY: Smell their breath.

MARK: What?

BETSY: Just do it!

(He does.)

MARK: Smells like almonds. That's weird. Dad hates almonds.

BETSY: I knew it! Cyanide poisoning!

NANCY: *(Suspiciously:)* And just how did you know that?

BETSY: Hey, I read!

AMY: Omigosh! It must have been the tea. *(To Nancy, eyes narrowing:)* And you made sure you cleaned up the cups, didn't you?

NANCY: Yeah? Well, who made the tea?

AMY: With you right there watching me!

(Mary puts her fingers in her mouth and makes a loud whistle. [Again, if the actress can't do this, she can make a loud noise in some other way.] Silence. All eyes on Mary.)

MARY: Just shut up, both of you! It wasn't you!

AMY: What? How do you know?

ANTHONY: Because we figured it out! Show them, Mary.

MARY: We found the answer in here.

(She plunks the scrapbook on a table and opens it up.)

NANCY: That's Mom's old scrapbook, from when we were little.

MARY: Take a look at this picture.

(Everyone except Betsy crowds around to look.)

NANCY: That's Tessie. Just before she disappeared.

MARY: Exactly. Now look closely. Who does she remind you of?

NANCY: *(Automatically:)* Whom.

(They all stare.)

AMY: Omigosh!

MARK: Wow!

NANCY: You're right. I should have seen it. I don't suppose Amy or Mark really remember her, they were so little. But I was eleven. I should have seen the resemblance!

BETSY: What? Who? What are you all talking about?

(They all look up. Blackout. Music may play to indicate the passage of time.)

(Lights up on the living room. It is midday. Nancy is seated with a book in her lap. Mary and Anthony stand near the exit to the front entrance. Amy stands near the exit to the kitchen. All four speak unnaturally loudly and a little artificially.)

MARY: Uncle Mark is out in the shed, doing something to the generator. I think he's got Betsy with him.

NANCY: That's nice.

ANTHONY: Mary and I are going out there to help them.

NANCY: All right.

AMY: I'm going to be in the kitchen, trying to fix dinner. Nobody bother me, okay, or I'll never manage it.

(She exits toward the kitchen.)

MARY: Will you be all right here all by yourself, Aunt Nancy?

NANCY: Oh, I'm sure I will. I don't suppose the mad murderer will get me right here in the middle of the living room.

ANTHONY: Well, okay then. See you later.

(Mary and Anthony exit toward the front entrance. We hear the ostentatiously loud sound of the door opening and closing. Nancy continues to read her book. Pause.)

(A cloaked figure enters stealthily from the bedrooms. Its face is obscured so we can't see who it is. It moves to the fireplace and picks up an iron poker. Then it moves behind Nancy and winds up to swing for her head.)

MARK: *(Off:)* Stop right there!

(Mark appears in the entrance from the kitchen. The cloaked figure freezes. Mary and Anthony appear in a window, or two windows. [NOTE: if you don't have practical windows in your set, they could appear instead in the entrance from the front entrance, behind Mark. But windows are more fun.])

MARY: We see you, too!

ANTHONY: You can't possibly get away!

(Mark moves to the figure and grabs it firmly. Mary and Anthony swarm through the windows [or from the front entrance]. Mary snatches the poker from the figure as Nancy leaps to her feet.)

MARY: I'll take that.

NANCY: And now let's get rid of that cloak!

(She sweeps the cloak off the struggling figure, revealing – Collette!)

ANTHONY: Collette!

MARY: Just as we suspected!

(Betsy and Amy enter from the kitchen.)

BETSY: Is it her?

NANCY: She.

BETSY: Whatever.

MARK: *(To Collette:)* Sit down right here and quit squirming! I've got a poker and I'm willing to use it!

(She does, reluctantly and with her eyes on the poker.)

MARY: *(To Betsy:)* Yes, it's Collette.

COLLETTE: *(In a cheesy French accent:)* But...you! You're supposed to be outside wiz ze generator! *(To Nancy, accusingly:)* You were supposed to be alone!

MARY: Merely a clever ruse to lure you out.

ANTHONY: It was Mary's idea.

COLLETTE: I knew I should have smozered you clever-britches keeds first!

BETSY: Collette! But you're dead!

AMY: Evidently not.

BETSY: But how?

COLLETTE: Very simply. As you know, I grew up in a traveling carnival.

BETSY: So?

MARY: I'll give you a hint: think Harry Houdini.

BETSY: Harry who?

COLLETTE: Precisely. Ze great 'Arry 'Oudini could 'old 'is breaz for minutes at a time. I learn ze trick from my carnival foster parents. I was ze magician's assistant. We 'ad a spectacular act. I would 'old my breaz and slow my 'eartbeat, so I appeared to be dead. We would even ask for a volunteer from ze audience—a doctor, if zere was one—to check my breazing and pulse. Zen my foster fazzer would cast a spell—wiz smoke and boomings—and I would come back to life. Eet was magnifique!

BETSY: Your foster father? But what happened to your real parents?

AMY: She killed them.

BETSY: What?!

MARY: Isn't that right, Collette? Or should I say, Aunt Tessie?

BETSY: Tessie? You mean the little girl who disappeared in Paris?

COLLETTE: Yes! Ze clever-britches ees right! I am Tessie Hopkins!

MARK: Of course you are! It was obvious once these "clever-britches" showed us those old scrapbooks.

MARY: It was really Uncle Mark who gave us the idea.

MARK: I did?

ANTHONY: What you said about the long-lost heir. Only you were talking about Betsy.

MARY: And you were only joking. But I admit I did think it might be Betsy for a while. She's the right age. That's why I wanted to see the scrapbooks.

MARK: But why, Tessie? Why?

COLLETTE: Well, I will tell. Seence all ees up wiz me, I see, I will tell. Picture to yourselves. Zere I am—a sweet leetle girl of four—on vacation wiz my family in Paris. Zere ees a carnival next door to ze 'otel, and in zis carnival ees a magician's act, n'est-ce pas?

NANCY: Yes, I remember that magician. We saw his act the day before you disappeared. He was very good.

COLLETTE: Yes, well, picture my fascination. Een ze act, ze great magician made a lady vanish, no? And I, leetle Tessie, burned to know 'ow it was done.

NANCY: *(To the others:)* She did always love magic. She was always trying to pull card tricks on Artie and me, and Mom and Dad. She wasn't very good at it.

COLLETTE: *(Angrily:)* I was four!

NANCY: Fair enough. Go on.

COLLETTE: As I say, I 'ad to know 'ow the lady was vanished. So I sneaked out of my room at ze 'otel and into ze magician's tent. And zere I found ze magical cabinet in which ze lady poofed. I climbed in. You must remember, I was a very curious four-year-old. I climbed in, and — poof!

AMY: Poof?

COLLETTE: *(Firmly:)* Poof. I was vanished!

BETSY: No!

COLLETTE: Oui. Eet was only a 'idden compartment, of course. But I could not get out. Zat very night ze carnival moved on, wiz leetle Tessie along for ze ride.

BETSY: How terrible!

COLLETTE: Two days later, zat magician got a beeg surprise. 'E makes one lady disappear — so far so good. And zen, to 'is surprise, 'e makes <u>two</u> ladies reappear!

AMY: But why didn't they bring you home again?

COLLETTE: Zey tried, of course. But you see, I was so young. I could not remember my last name, nor where ze 'otel was. And ze carnival folk were not keen to go back to Paris. Eet seems zere was some contratemps — somezing about some not-zo-nice tricks by ze fortune teller. But I was not worried. I knew my muzzer and fazzer would never stop looking until zey find me. Only I was wrong.

NANCY: You weren't! They looked for you for years!

COLLETTE: If zey had — listen... *(In unaccented American English:)* ...do you mind if I drop the French accent?

AMY: *(Dryly:)* Oh, is that what it was?

COLLETTE: If they had really looked for me, they would have found me.

NANCY: But they did!

AMY: They were devastated! Even I remember that, and I was five.

COLLETTE: Oh, I'm sure they went through the motions. It might not look right otherwise. Finally, the Magnificent Maestro —

AMY: The who?

COLLETTE: That was his stage name. Finally he sort of adopted me, he and his wife, Marie. And they brought me up in the carnival and taught me all the tricks. I was a natural, needless to say.

AMY: I'll bet.

COLLETTE: It wasn't a bad life, really, but all I could think of was being rescued. Until it was obvious no one cared. Then all I could think of was revenge.

NANCY: But didn't you try to find out who you were? When you were older, I mean.

COLLETTE: Oh, I did figure it out, of course. How it happened was this. Usually, when the carnival stopped at a place, we all slept in the tents and trailers. But one day when I was about nine, we stopped at this run-down town where the wagons were all infested with fleas. We got halfway to our next destination in Nice before we realized it.

BETSY: Ugh!

COLLETTE: Yes, it was pretty bad. So we wound up staying in a hotel while everything was fumigated. And there was a television in my room. I loved television when I was little, but I hadn't seen it in years, so I put it on. And there were dear Mom and Dad, telling the world they were stopping their search and giving up little Tessie for dead. And it showed snapshots of the rest of the family, and how rich and coddled they all were. After that, I was more determined than ever to destroy you all. I just didn't know how until you... *(To Amy:)* ...showed up in Paris. It was perfect. Here was this rich, up-and-coming fashion model, living the glamorous life in Paris —

AMY: Trust me, it's not as glamorous as it looks.

COLLETTE: — and you had no idea who I was.

AMY: How could I? I was only five when you vanished!

COLLETTE: So I cobbled together some fake references and sweet-talked you into bringing me home.

NANCY: If you'd only said...

COLLETTE: Do you have any idea what it was like, working as a maid for the family that forgot me? Do you? Slaving and bowing?

MARK: We treated you very well! Like family! Well, okay, Aunt Gloria didn't. But the rest of us —

COLLETTE: Oh, sure, you all gave me nice presents on my birthday — didn't that tip you off, by the way? No, of course not. You were all too preoccupied living the rich life! It was torture, but I did it. For <u>five years</u>! And I waited for my chance. When dear old Dad insisted on having this family gathering so late in the season, I saw my opportunity. It was me who wrote that note about not bringing any electronics along, by the way.

NANCY: I thought that didn't quite sound like Dad. He always wrote in iambic pentameter, and that one was in trochaic tetrameter.

MARK: *(Astounded, to Nancy:)* How do you <u>know</u> stuff like that?

AMY: A better question would be "why?"

COLLETTE: Then it was a simple matter of faking my own death. I knew once you had me stashed in my own room, you'd never look in there again. What could a dead woman do? And the phone was there, so you could all wake me up in the middle of the night to demand hot milk —

AMY: *(In protest:)* Never once...

COLLETTE: So I was all set. I just started picking you off one by one. The phone calls were my master stroke. That threw you all off the scent for a while.

BETSY: But how could you be sure there'd be an avalanche, for heaven's sake?

MARY: Oh, she did that herself. Didn't we tell you? Anthony and I figured that out ages ago.

COLLETTE: Exactly. I knew where those old fireworks were stored. Who do you think had to shove 'em in there in the first place?

NANCY: It's diabolical!

MARK: And I suppose once we were all dead, you were

planning on suddenly "discovering" that you were the long-lost heir to the Hopkins Greetings fortune?

COLLETTE: Naturally. It was only fair, since I didn't get to enjoy it while you were alive. I knew my fingerprints must be on file with my birth certificate. All I had to do was fly back to France, and then wander into the U.S. Embassy. I'd have been devastated to learn my family were all dead—but I'd have spent the money anyway.

MARY: But there's one thing I don't understand. How did you plan to get away? I mean, you're snowed in here, too.

(We hear the sound of a helicopter, distant but growing nearer.)

COLLETTE: Oh, I had that all worked out. In fact, I think I hear my ride coming now. I guess I'll be going to a slightly different place than I thought. If I'm not mistaken, that will be the authorities. They were supposed to find the faithful maid, frantic after the family slaughtered one another over their silly money. I thought I'd have more time when I called them.

NANCY: You called them? But there are no phones!

COLLETTE: You're not very smart for someone who knows about iambic pentameter, are you?

(She reaches into her bodice, or a pocket or something. The helicopter has grown quite loud.)

AMY: Stop her! She's going for a gun!

MARY: *(Not even a little bit alarmed:)* I bet she isn't.

(Collette pulls out a cell phone, which she flaunts. In the background, we hear the sound of the helicopter powering down.)

COLLETTE: I wasn't about to pay attention to fussy old Daddy's rules. Especially since I wrote them myself.

(A loud banging on the outside door.)

OFFICER ONE: *(Off:)* Anyone in here?

SHARON: *(Off:)* Mary? Anthony?

OFFICER TWO: *(Off:)* Break it down!

(A loud crash off. Enter two police officers, OFFICER ONE and OFFICER TWO, followed, and, indeed, outpaced, by Anthony and Mary's mother, SHARON.)

MARY & ANTHONY: Mom!

(They rush to Sharon and a three-way hug ensues.)

OFFICER ONE: What's going on? We got a report that the whole family was dead.

OFFICER TWO: There are six corpses on the front porch! *(To Mark, who still hovers over Collette with the poker:)* What's the deal with the poker?

MARK: It's a long story. Allow me to present my little sister, Miss Tessie Hopkins, AKA Collette Miraux. She's responsible for the bodies out front, I'm sorry to say.

OFFICER ONE: *(To Collette:)* Is that so, miss?

COLLETTE: *(Defiant, and back to "French":)* Yes! I won't give you ze satisfaction of denying eet! Not so you can lock me in ze dungeons and beat ze truz out of me wiz your 'oses of rubber! I am geelty!

OFFICER TWO: Listen, sister, we don't do that kind of thing in this country. Maybe in Italy or Bulgaria or wherever you're from...

(Officer Two takes out handcuffs and snaps them on Collette.)

COLLETTE: *(Furious:)* Italy! Zees is a <u>French</u> accent!

OFFICER ONE: *(To Mark:)* How did you figure it out?

MARK: Well, actually...

BETSY: Hey, wait a minute! Why do you assume the <u>man</u> figured it out?

OFFICER ONE: *(To Betsy:)* Oh, excuse me, miss. So it was you who figured it out, huh?

BETSY: No, it wasn't! I'm just saying...

NANCY: Actually, Officer, it was these two.

(She moves to Mary and Anthony and puts one hand on each head.)

OFFICER ONE: Izzat so? Hey, nice going, kids.

OFFICER TWO: You two ever think of joining the police force when you get older?

SHARON: Don't give them any ideas!

MARY: *(Suddenly bashful:)* It was nothing, really.

ANTHONY: *(Shrugging elaborately:)* Yeah, it was pretty obvious. Only sometimes grown-ups don't think too good.

OFFICER ONE: *(Looking pointedly at Collette:)* In my experience, that's very true.

OFFICER TWO: Yeah. Well, since we got a confession, I don't guess we need to take up a whole lot more of everyone's time. Thing is, we got that call that everyone was dead, so we've got lots of body bags and stretchers but not so many seats in the helicopter. You mind if we take the suspect and the deceased out of here and send another chopper for the rest of you?

NANCY: *(Shrugging:)* We've been here this long—another couple more hours won't kill us.

BETSY: Not if you take <u>her</u> with you, they won't.

OFFICER TWO: Oh, don't you worry about that. Come on,

you. I mean, miss.

(The two Officers escort Collette towards the door. Just before they're out of sight, Collette stops.)

COLLETTE: Wait!

(They do, and she turns to face the others.)

SEVERAL OTHERS: What?!

COLLETTE: *(In regular English:)* One of my fondest memories from before this family abandoned me —

NANCY: Hey!

MARK: Let it go, Nancy.

COLLETTE: —was watching television, surrounded by my stuffed animals and my dolls. There was this one show — I don't really remember much, but there was a talking dog, I know. And there was a line I always wanted to say — and I guess this is my last chance.

AMY: Oh, boy — here it comes.

(Collette points a shaking finger at Mary and Anthony. Her accent is back.)

COLLETTE: And I would 'ave got away wiz eet, too, eef eet wasn't for you meddling keeds!

(Blackout. End of play.)

The Author Speaks

What inspired you to write this play?
One season, all three of the publishers that handle my work
put out calls for mystery plays. Since I've always been an avid
reader of whodunits of all types, I thought why not? But
because I have also always focused on writing plays for young
people, I wanted to feature young people as the protagonists.
So I came up with the idea of spoofing a favorite genre—old
fashioned, ultra-civilized English whodunits of the Agatha
Christie, Ngaio Marsh and Dorothy Sayers school—but setting
it in present-day America and having the mystery unraveled
by kids. I chose the cliché "since we're isolated here in this (fill
in the location), the killer must be one of us" structure in part
because it *is* a cliché, but mostly because it makes staging
easier, since there's only one location.

**Was the structure or other elements of the play influenced
by any other work?**
Obviously it's very consciously modeled on the structure of
the novels it spoofs.

**Have you dealt with the same theme in other works that you
have written?**
Apart from the theme of kids making things happen, rather
than being passive "victims," not really. This play is a
departure for me in several ways. I've never written a mystery
before and I don't usually do spoofs of any variety.

**What writers have had the most profound effect on your
style?**
I am influenced by writers who use words well (at least in the
sense that I *try* to emulate them—how successful I am is for
others to judge). P. G. Wodehouse is a favorite. Even if his
plots had been deadly dull (they weren't, by and large), his
novels and short stories would still be amongst the funniest

things ever written in English. Taking on a whodunit for the first time, I suppose I was influenced by those in that genre who have that gift. Rex Stout and Charlotte MacLeod leap to mind — their stories couldn't be more different, but they share the ability to effortlessly bend the language to their will, and both are uproariously funny even when the situations about which they write are not.

What do you hope to achieve with this work?
I hope I have written a play that performers will enjoy performing and audiences will enjoy auditing. (See what I did there? I love words.) Seriously, though, not every play has to be about some massively important social idea. There is, or ought to be, a place for art for art's sake. I hope folks enjoy my work — simple as that.

What were the biggest challenges involved in the writing of this play?
I usually struggle to answer this question, but for this play it's an easy one: structuring the plot. I had to figure out not only who actually did the crime and how, but how and why folks would suspect others in turn, how the "clues" that would eventually lead to the solution would be discovered, and what "red herrings" to introduce. I don't usually work from an outline, but for this play it was essential. Even so, I expect actors and audiences will find plenty of holes in the plot.

What are the most common mistakes that occur in productions of your work?
I am rarely disappointed when I see a production of one of my plays. I've never seen a perfect one, of course (how boring would that be?), but I usually come away feeling well served by the cast and director. Still, if I had to pick one issue, it would be timing. I am a musician as well as a playwright, and I tend to use words in part for their rhythmic value. If actors break up sentences in order to "act" (or, worse, paraphrase

them), the rhythm is lost and a scene can drag. It's not about going fast, though that's part of it. It's about trusting the words to do their job. That's especially important in a play as stylized as this one.

What inspired you to become a playwright?
I became a playwright because it was hard. True story. In high school I gravitated towards the theatre in large part because it was the only thing in that school that I found challenging (and trust me, I was a *bad* actor). Once I had been hooked by the theatre as a broad discipline, I discovered theatre with young people basically by accident, when I took a job directing a high school play. I took the job because it was a directing gig, not because it involved working with young people, but I was instantly hooked. Then, when I went to grad school for theatre with young people, I was asked to choose among three areas on which to focus — directing, teaching, or playwriting — and I made a conscious decision to go with the one I knew least about. I figured I'd learn more that way. And, again, I was hooked.

How did you research the subject?
Unless you count devouring an average of two or three crime novels a week for most of my adult life, I didn't.

Are any characters modeled after real life or historical figures?
My young characters are always modeled to one extent or another on actual kids I have known. I'm not going to tell you who, but I'll bet they'd recognize themselves. I'm sure some of the adults in this play also have living influences, but I didn't do it on purpose. I don't know anyone who always talks in verse — though I certainly know of many politicians who always talk in gibberish.

What is your writing process?

Usually I just think of a situation and some characters and start writing to see where they go. I let the characters tell me what the play is about. This play was different, because it had to be so carefully, even mathematically structured. I had the entire plot worked out on paper before I wrote a single line of dialogue (though the characters, once they came to life, often suggested improvements to the original outline).

Shakespeare gave advice to the players in *Hamlet*; if you could give advice to your cast what would it be?

Don't be funny. Much of the humor in this play comes from the fact that the characters remain basically calm and civilized even when they know there's a killer among them—and when they do go over the edge, it's usually to attack the wrong person. That will be funnier if it's played straight.

By the way, I have always been skeptical of the above statement. Shakespeare is not a character in *Hamlet*. Hamlet, not Shakespeare, gives advice to the players in *Hamlet*. It is typically assumed that Hamlet is in this case a mouthpiece for Shakespeare himself, but I've never been completely convinced—especially since Hamlet says many other things elsewhere in the play that Shakespeare almost certainly didn't think. In the scene in question, Shakespeare is obviously taking an opportunity to take jabs at other producers, but I think he may be taking a few at himself as well. More broadly, I think it's dangerous to assume that the words that come out of any character's mouth necessarily reflect the opinions of the playwright. If that were true, how could anyone write bad guys? (Which is my way of saying that the opinions expressed by the characters in this play, especially Artie and Virginia, are not necessarily those of the playwright, his family, or the Commonwealth of Massachusetts.)

About the Author

Matt Buchanan is a New England-based professional playwright, composer and director specializing in theatre with and for young people. His more than two dozen published plays and musicals have been performed across the United States and on every continent but Antarctica. He has directed more than one hundred productions with young casts and is the author of *Directing Kids: A Comprehensive How-To Manual for Directors of Plays and Musicals with Casts of Young People from a Veteran Drama Teacher and Director,* published by YouthPLAYS. He is also an accomplished musician and multi-instrumentalist. Matt has a BA in Music from Harvard College and an MFA in Child Drama from the University of Texas at Austin. His website is www.childdrama.com.

About YouthPLAYS

YouthPLAYS (www.youthplays.com) is a publisher of award-winning professional dramatists and talented new discoveries, each with an original theatrical voice, and all dedicated to expanding the vocabulary of theatre for young actors and audiences. On our website you'll find one-act and full-length plays and musicals for teen and pre-teen (and even college) actors, as well as duets and monologues for competition. Many of our authors' works have been widely produced at high schools and middle schools, youth theatres and other TYA companies, both amateur and professional, as well as at elementary schools, camps, churches and other institutions serving young audiences and/or actors worldwide. Most are intended for performance by young people, while some are intended for adult actors performing for young audiences.

YouthPLAYS was co-founded by professional playwrights Jonathan Dorf and Ed Shockley. It began merely as an additional outlet to market their own works, which included a substantial body of award-winning published and unpublished plays and musicals. Those interested in their published plays were directed to the respective publishers' websites, and unpublished plays were made available in electronic form. But when they saw the desperate need for material for young actors and audiences—coupled with their experience that numerous quality plays for young people weren't finding a home—they made the decision to represent the work of other playwrights as well. Dozens and dozens of authors are now members of the YouthPLAYS family, with scripts available both electronically and in traditional acting editions. We continue to grow as we look for exciting and challenging plays and musicals for young actors and audiences.

About ProduceaPlay.com

Let's put up a play! Great idea! But producing a play takes time, energy and knowledge. While finding the necessary time and energy is up to you, ProduceaPlay.com is a website designed to assist you with that third element: knowledge.

Created by YouthPLAYS' co-founders, Jonathan Dorf and Ed Shockley, ProduceaPlay.com serves as a resource for producers at all levels as it addresses the many facets of production. As Dorf and Shockley speak from their years of experience (as playwrights, producers, directors and more), they are joined by a group of award-winning theatre professionals and experienced teachers from the world of academic theatre, all making their expertise available for free in the hope of helping this and future generations of producers, whether it's at the school or university level, or in community or professional theatres.

The site is organized into a series of major topics, each of which has its own page that delves into the subject in detail, offering suggestions and links for further information. For example, Publicity covers everything from Publicizing Auditions to How to Use Social Media to Posters to whether it's worth hiring a publicist. Casting details Where to Find the Actors, How to Evaluate a Resume, Callbacks and even Dealing with Problem Actors. You'll find guidance on your Production Timeline, The Theater Space, Picking a Play, Budget, Contracts, Rehearsing the Play, The Program, House Management, Backstage, and many other important subjects.

The site is constantly under construction, so visit often for the latest insights on play producing, and let it help make your play production dreams a reality.

More from YouthPLAYS

The Unscary Ghost by Matt Buchanan
Comedy. 40-50 minutes. 5+ females, 3+ males (13-30+ performers possible).

Loosely based on Oscar Wilde's *The Canterville Ghost*. When the Otis family moves into the old Victorian home in Canterville, Ohio, they soon learn that it's haunted—by a ghost who can't scare anyone. The jaded, modern family alternately taunts and tries to exploit the unfortunate ghost, Simon Canter, even trying to get a spot on the hit TV show, *America's Most Haunted*. Only the oldest daughter, Ginny, seems to care for or understand poor Simon. Can she help him find peace in this zany but touching show for the whole family?

Dancing With Myself by Leanne Griffin
Dramedy. 35-45 minutes. 7 females.

Goth Girl. Moody Chick. Gamer. Cheerleader. New Kid. Jock. Nerd. Seven high school girls and the labels they've been forced to wear. But in this innovative, award-winning dramedy, whether it's sports or a sleepover or the classroom or a school dance or the ups and downs of daily life, they'll use music as their inspiration to break free of the stereotypes and discover the unique identity they each possess.

How the Elephant Got His Trunk by Cary Nothnagel
Comedy. 25-35 minutes. 7-17 females, 5-12 males (8-24 performers possible).

When Elton's questions become too much for his family and neighbors, the young elephant sets out to find his own answers. But it's said that curiosity killed the cat, and it may not be healthy for elephants either. Will Elton's insatiable inquisitiveness make him wiser, or will it make him dinner?

The Ghost Moments by Randy Wyatt

Drama. 45-70 minutes. 1-10 females, 1-5 males (2-15 performers total).

We all have ghosts that haunt us. Some are literal: Matty tries to rid his sister's apartment of a spirit that may or may not be there, Zachary prepares his bunker for the zombie apocalypse. Others are metaphorical: Marianne's absent father, Caroline's memories of water, Carver's secret powers. As we witness hauntings and exorcisms through a series of monologues, this group of characters and their loves, longings, joy and pain, will haunt us long after the curtain falls.

The Superhero Ultraferno by Don Zolidis

Comedy. 100-110 minutes. 6-50 females, 6-50 males (12-90+ performers).

Now that nerds have taken over the world, it's imperative that all popular kids learn everything they can about comic book superheroes. Join two nerds and a crack team of actors as they race hilariously through the world of tights-wearing crimefighters, from the 1960s TV Batman to the soap opera insanity of the Fantastic Four to a bizarre, German opera of Spiderman. Also available as a one-act.

4 A.M. by Jonathan Dorf (book) and Alison Wood (music and lyrics)

Musical. 75-80 minutes. 4+ males, 4+ females (8-40+ performers possible).

What's it like to be awake when your world is asleep? Meet early morning joggers, a lonely radio DJ, a modern Romeo and Juliet, the writer of a most unusual letter, and numerous other teens. Through songs, scenes and monologues, they'll survive lonely nights and sleepovers, discover whether the Monster Under the Bed is real and maybe even find an answer to that all-important question: "Is anybody out there?"

Made in the USA
Columbia, SC
19 November 2017